ERIC HUANG

Oh No They DIDN'T

REMARKABLE WOMEN

Blast off with these remarkable women!

ILLUSTRATED BY
SAM CALDWELL

words&pictures

First published in 2025 by words & pictures,
an imprint of The Quarto Group.
1 Triptych Place, London,
SE1 9SH, United Kingdom.
T (0)20 7700 6700 F (0)20 7700 8066
www.quarto.com

Copyeditor: Nancy Dickmann
Assistant Editor: Jackie Lui
Project Editor: Alice Hobbs
Designer: Kathryn Davies
Production Manager: Nikki Ingram
Creative Director: Malena Stojić
Associate Publisher: Holly Willsher

A catalogue record for this book is available from the British Library.

ISBN: 978-0-7112-9288-8

Manufactured in Guangdong, China TT102024

9 8 7 6 5 4 3 2 1

ERIC HUANG

Oh No They Didn't

REMARKABLE WOMEN

FASCINATING FACTS YOU NEVER KNEW ABOUT AMAZING WOMEN!

ILLUSTRATED BY
SAM CALDWELL

words&pictures

CONTENTS

We're cleared for take off.

INTRODUCTION...06

LEGENDS...08
Universal Mothers
Fearless Fighters
Wonderfully Wicked
Mighty Mortals

GENIUSES..16
Mathematical Masterminds
Ingenious Innovators
Medical Masterminds
Galactic Greats

CREATIVES...24
Amazing Artists
Wise Wordsmiths
Dazzling Designers
Musical Maestros

SUPERSTARS...................32
Dazzling Divas
Leading Ladies
Screen Sensations
Media Moguls

She's out of this world!

Meet some high flyers, change-makers, and record-breakers.

LEADERS..40
Leading Lights
Formidable First Ladies
Regal Royalty
Political Powerhouses

TRAILBLAZERS..48
Fearless Firsts
Wilderness Warriors
Daring Defenders
Sport Stars

TIMELINE..56
MAP..58
GLOSSARY...60
ABOUT THE AUTHOR & ILLUSTRATOR.....64

Ladies always rise above.

INTRODUCTION

Remarkable women have been at the forefront of history. They've changed the world and are leading the way to our future. Long ago, legendary women were worshipped as gods and honoured as heroes.

More recently, trailblazing women forged new paths for all to follow, tearing down obstacles along the way. Many women were the geniuses behind technological breakthroughs and imaginative inventions that greatly improved our lives. They're the superstars we listen to and watch on screens of all sizes, the leaders who inspire us and the bosses breaking through the glass ceiling.

How much do you really know about the remarkable women who've shaped our world? Of course, every one of them knew what they wanted to do from an early age. They always had a clear path. They're consistently confident and reliably strong. **And all of them easily persevered in the face of discrimination. . . didn't they?**

OH NO THEY DIDN'T!

TURN THE PAGE to read about the lives and accomplishments of **over 50 women.**

Meet world leaders and activists, athletes and musicians, scientists and business executives, and many more.

Computer programmer

Biochemist

Artist

Activist

FOLLOW THE DIVERSITY OF PATHS THAT LED TO THEIR SUCCESSES – which often weren't straight lines, but rather meandering and totally unexpected!

LEGENDS
UNIVERSAL MOTHERS

The legends and lore of bygone civilizations are full of epic tales, magic and gods. Our ancient ancestors always gave the highest honours to male gods. . . didn't they?

OH NO THEY DIDN'T!

The Egyptian goddess **Isis** was queen of the universe. She was one of the most important gods – not just in Egypt, but throughout the ancient Mediterranean. There was no greater sorcerer than Isis, who was a healer and had power over death itself! As the divine mother of the Egyptian kings (known as pharaohs), it was to Isis that people turned for protection.

Yaas queen!

Isis

There are powerful goddesses in other cultures, too.

Oshun, a water goddess of the Yoruba people in West Africa, is one of the divine beings who created the world and cared for human beings! Amaterasu is from Japan. Like Isis, she's the mother of kings. People worshipped Amaterasu because she was royalty. . . didn't they?

OH NO THEY DIDN'T

Amaterasu is a sun goddess. Without her, there would be no warmth or light for growing food.

Oshun

Amaterasu

Did you know that Amaterasu has two younger brothers? Tsukuyomi is the moon god and Susanoo is a trickster god of storms. Tsukuyomi behaved so badly at a banquet once that his older sister hasn't spoken to him since – that's why the moon and sun don't share the sky. Susanoo also behaved badly, leaving a poop on his sister's throne! Amaterasu was so offended that she shut herself in a cave, plunging the world into darkness. It was only after Susanoo was kicked out of Heaven that Amaterasu brought the sun back.

FEARLESS FIGHTERS

Ancient cultures only worshipped female gods as mother figures. . . didn't they?

OH NO THEY DIDN'T!

She's the real Lion King.

Many goddesses were formidable warriors. **Ishtar**, also known as Inanna, was honoured as the queen of heaven by the ancient peoples of Mesopotamia. She's often shown dressed in battle-ready armour with lions at her side as symbols of power.

Ishtar was an important divinity who controlled the harvest, rain and thunder.

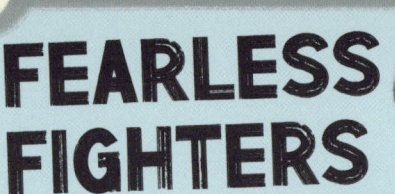

Ishtar

Another goddess associated with war was Freyja, worshipped by the Norse people, who we sometimes call Vikings. She's famous because she ruled Asgard, the land of the gods, as the wife of the god Odin. . . didn't she?

OH NO SHE DIDN'T!

Odin was one of the main Norse gods. His wife was Frigg, a goddess similar to **Freyja**. Freyja, however, wasn't just an immortal sidekick. Love and beauty were her domain, and so were war and battle. Freyja chose which worthy warriors would live in her enchanted land, Folkvangr, after they were killed in battle.

Did you know that Freyja rode a chariot pulled by flying cats? What a purr-fect way to travel! Sometimes Freyja is called Queen of the Valkyries, an all-female company of armoured soldiers who rode winged horses. It was their job to select the bravest of fallen warriors and lead them to a magical hall of the gods called Valhalla.

freyja

Cat-apulting through the clouds!

Athena was an Ancient Greek goddess of war, fighting alongside chosen warriors with supreme skill. One of her symbols was the owl, a bird as wise as she was.

Athena

Did you know that Athena was also the goddess of crafts? She was the ultimate divinity – incredibly strong as well as super-smart!

WONDERFULLY WICKED

Legendary goddesses ruled over love, healing and harvests. They only dedicated themselves to doing good. . . didn't they?

OH NO THEY DIDN'T!

Many women from ancient myths were delightfully devious. **Lamashtu** from Mesopotamia was the mother of demons. She was known by seven different magical names and was the creator of nightmares.

Lamashtu

Ala is the name given to a female demon from Slavic folklore – more than one are called 'ale'. An ala can appear as a black wind, a raven or a woman, and they're to blame for bad weather. But did you know that ale are afraid of dragons? Dragons chase them away to protect harvests.

In Ancient Greek stories, Medusa was a beautiful woman with snakes for hair. Anyone who looked at her turned into stone. . . didn't they?

OH NO THEY DIDN'T!

Medusa

At least, not quite. Looking at her from behind would be safe – it was eye contact that turned people into stone. The hero Perseus defeated her by looking at her reflection in his shield.

Did you know that **Medusa** was once human? Her hair turned into snakes after she offended Athena. Talk about the ultimate bad-hair day! Today, Medusa is often seen as a symbol of those who have been wronged.

Legends are full of wicked witches. All of them were bad and only did evil things. . . didn't they?

OH NO THEY DIDN'T!

Circe

Lets get out of here!

Circe was a sorceress, the daughter of a sun god. She could transform men into animals, but she also used her magical powers to help the Greek heroes Jason and Odysseus on their quests. Although Circe appeared in many stories as a wicked witch, she's applauded today as a strong woman who shaped her own destiny.

13

MIGHTY MORTALS

Many female figures from legend were goddesses, but mortal women in legend were just ordinary. They stayed home and avoided adventure. . . didn't they?

Bring it!

Hua Mulan

OH NO THEY DIDN'T!

Hua Mulan is a Chinese folk hero who took her elderly father's place in the army to defend her country. Because women weren't allowed to be soldiers, she disguised herself as a man. Although still a teen, Mulan proved to be a skilled fighter and won many battles.

Hua Mulan probably never really existed, but there is a real historical figure from France in the 1400s who also dressed as a man to fight a war. Everyone thought Joan of Arc was a man. . . didn't they?

OH NO THEY DIDN'T!

Joan of Arc

Pocahontas was an Indigeneous person from the Powhatan tribe, who lived almost 500 years ago in the Americas. Her real-life adventures have been turned into legendary stories. Pocahontas's father, Wahunsenacawh, was chief of the Powhatans. Pocahontas served her people as a princess. . . didn't she?

OH NO SHE DIDN'T!

The concept of royalty didn't exist in Powhatan culture. Her father was an elected ruler of the Powhatan people, so **Pocahontas** wasn't a princess. However, she played a key role as an ambassador between cultures.

Pocahontas

As a girl, **Joan** heard divine voices that told her to join the army and fight for her country. Like Mulan, she wore men's clothing to fight – but this wasn't a disguise. A soldier's breeches and armour were more practical than a dress in battle. Everyone knew Joan was a woman and they were inspired by her bravery. She was only about seventeen when she first rode into battle!

Brave and battle ready!

With sensible shoes.

GENIUSES

$log e \frac{w_1 d}{w_1}$+

MATHEMATICAL MASTERMINDS

Some of the brightest mathematicians are women. Three African American women were critical to NASA's first crewed space flights in the 1960s.

Katherine Johnson, Dorothy Vaughan and Mary Jackson were hired to act as human computers. Computers back then were nowhere near as advanced as the ones we use today, so it was their job to be computers and perform the calculations that made space missions possible. Because they were so brilliant, the women quickly rose through the ranks. . . didn't they?

$$\frac{w_1}{w_{1,d}} \cdot \frac{y_d}{y} = \frac{w_{2,d}}{w_2}$$

Mary Jackson

Dorothy Vaughan

OH NO THEY DIDN'T!

It's not rocket science. . .it's rocket maths!

Katherine Johnson

Women were generally not credited for their contributions in those days. They had to fight for recognition. And because they were Black, **Johnson**, **Vaughan** and **Jackson** were segregated from their white co-workers. There were separate offices, toilets and eating areas for Black employees. All three mathematicians fought for important roles in NASA's space programme and helped other women carve out careers in science.

One small step for man, from many big contributions from women.

Did you know that the first computer programmer was a woman? Over 200 years ago, the mathematician **Ada Lovelace** worked on an early computer called the Analytical Engine. She wrote a program for the machine to compute a complex series of numbers. Lovelace was the first person to see the potential for computers to be more than number crunchers. She imagined computers of the future processing words, music and images. Sound familiar?

Ada Lovelace

Many modern mathematicians are women, but in ancient times, women stayed away from maths and science. . . didn't they?

OH NO THEY DIDN'T!

Hypatia was a mathematician, astronomer, and philosopher who lived over 1,500 years ago. She was one of the most highly regarded thinkers and made many contributions in mathematics, as well as astronomy and philosophy.

Hypatia

INGENIOUS INNOVATORS

The work of brilliant scientists over the centuries has led to our modern technology and conveniences. There were female inventors and thinkers, but men pioneered all the breakthroughs. . . didn't they?

OH NO THEY DIDN'T!

Polish-born French physicist **Marie Curie** was the first woman to win the prestigious Nobel Prize, an award for people who've made significant contributions to the world. She's also the first person in the world to win it twice! Her discoveries in radiation helped improve X-ray images and led to life-saving cancer treatments.

You won twice!

Marie Curie

Hedy Lamarr

THE INVENTOR OF WIFI

Did you know that an actress with a star on the Hollywood Walk of Fame was an inventor? **Hedy Lamarr** was a movie star from the Golden Age of Hollywood, but she was much more than her glamorous image. Lamarr was always interested in the inner working of machines and could speak four languages! She and a friend invented a telecommunications system that influenced mobile phone technology.

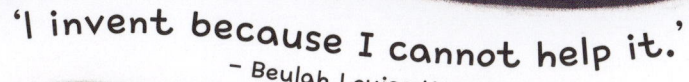

'I invent because I cannot help it.'
– Beulah Louise Henry

Women are behind a huge range of inventions. Did you know that the first windscreen wipers, life rafts, dishwashers, fire escapes, disposable nappies and chocolate chip cookies were all invented by women? The most famous female inventors were experts in their fields. They all made discoveries in one area of speciality. . . didn't they?

OH NO THEY DIDN'T!

Beulah Louise Henry was a prolific American inventor. She had 110 inventions, including an ice-cream maker, a hair curler, toys, a tin opener and numerous sewing devices. While all of these are household items, inventing them required Henry to have knowledge about a wide range of materials, theories and techniques. Talk about a hard worker!

MEDICAL MASTERMINDS

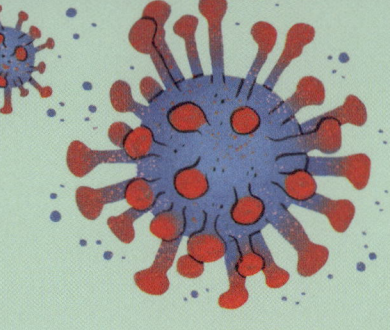

Sarah Gilbert is a pioneer in vaccinology. She led the team at Oxford University that created one of the first vaccines against COVID-19 – and continues her research to find a universal immunization against influenza. Gilbert always imagined a future as a vaccinologist. . . didn't she?

OH NO SHE DIDN'T!

Sarah Gilbert

Although **Gilbert** wanted to work in medicine since she was a young girl, she earned her PhD studying a yeast used for a variety of purposes by food and pharmaceutical companies. When Gilbert finished her doctorate, she worked as a researcher for a food and drink foundation. It wasn't until later that she began studying pathogens and infectious diseases.

Did you know that Gilbert is a mother to triplets? They all studied biochemistry!

Jennifer Doudna

Jennifer Doudna is a ground-breaking American biochemist. She and her partner, Emmanuelle Charpentier, developed CRISPR gene editing, an ingenious method to quickly and accurately cut and paste bits of DNA, the building blocks of life. The procedure is being used to create new treatments for a wide range of diseases and infections, as well as conditions ranging from cancer to blindness and diabetes.

Doudna grew up in Hawai'i, where the tropical flora and fauna of the island awakened her lifelong love of science. She received encouragement from everyone to pursue her dream of becoming a scientist. . . didn't she?

OH NO SHE DIDN'T!

Doudna's parents always supported her dreams, but a high school guidance counsellor told her, 'Women don't go into science'. Inspired by female scientists like her chemistry teacher and a researcher from the University of Hawai'i, Doudna ignored the bad advice to become a Nobel Prize-winning scientist. This woman didn't just go into science, she mastered it!

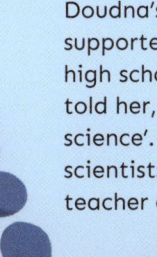

GALACTIC GREATS

Many women have participated in the exploration of space.

Italian astronaut **Samantha Cristoforetti** is the first European woman to command an expedition on the International Space Station (ISS). On one of her ISS missions, she stayed in space for 199 days and 16 hours, making her the record holder for the longest single space flight for a European astronaut!

Did you know that Samantha Cristoforetti is the first person ever to brew an espresso in space? The ISSpresso is a coffee machine designed for use in microgravity. Cristoforetti installed the machine on the International Space Station and whipped up a cosmic cuppa.

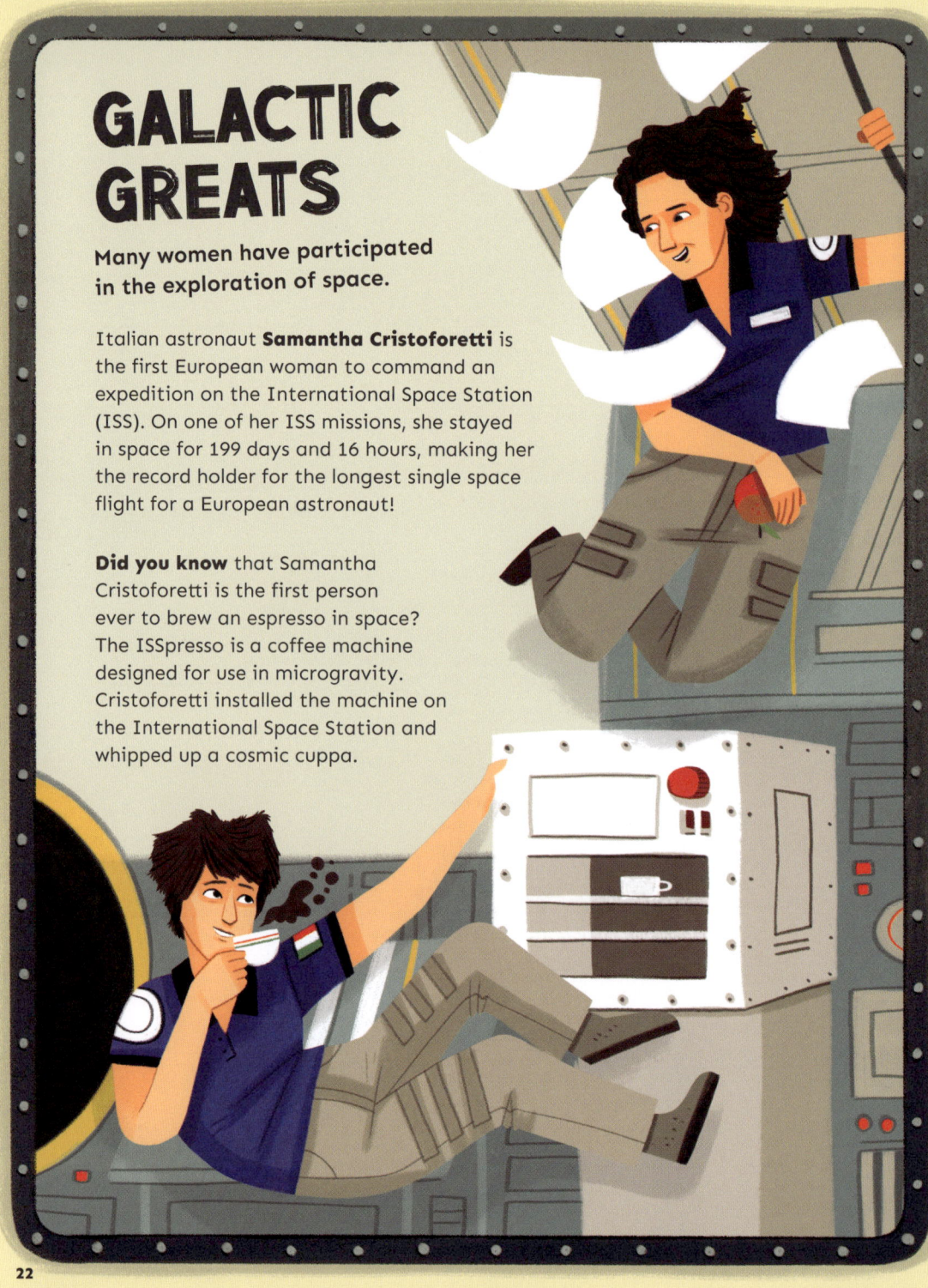

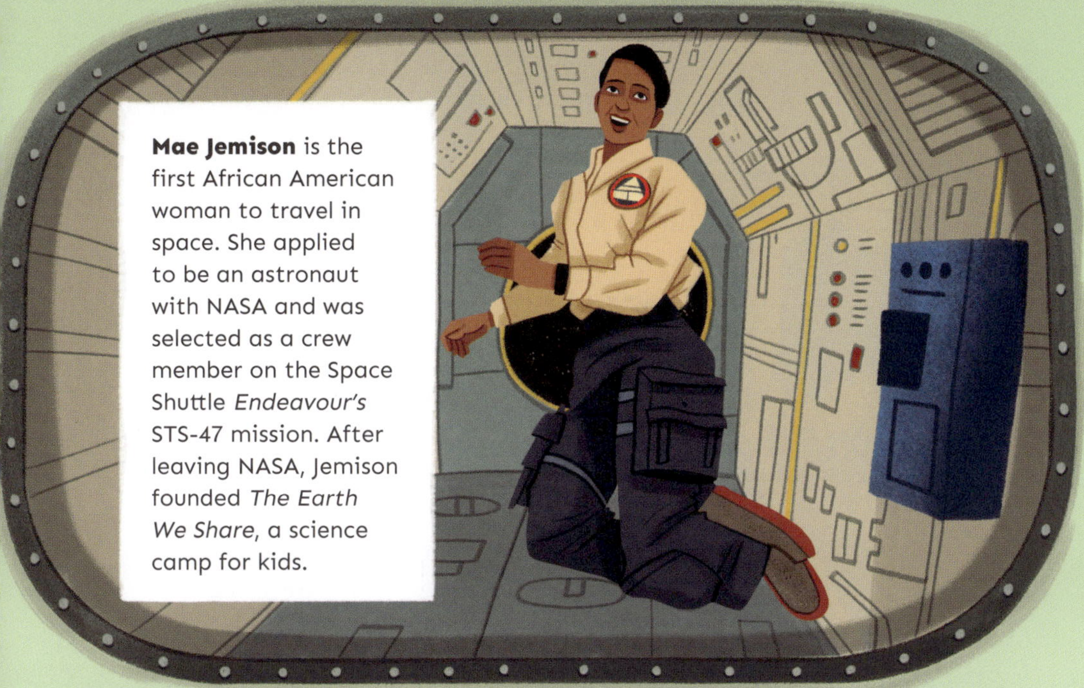

Mae Jemison is the first African American woman to travel in space. She applied to be an astronaut with NASA and was selected as a crew member on the Space Shuttle *Endeavour's* STS-47 mission. After leaving NASA, Jemison founded *The Earth We Share*, a science camp for kids.

Like most astronauts, Jemison loved science more than any other subject. . . didn't she?

OH NO SHE DIDN'T!

Jemison always loved science, but she had non-scientific interests as well. One of these was dance. Jemison studied many different forms of dance, from ballet to jazz, and was torn between pursuing a career in science and becoming a dancer. She ended up doing both! Jemison graduated from college with degrees in chemical engineering and African American studies, but she also took dance classes at the prestigious Alvin Ailey American Dance Theater while enrolled in medical school.

Did you know that Jemison is also a children's book author? Dancer, author, doctor, engineer, astronaut. Jemison's accomplishments are out of this world!

CREATIVES
AMAZING ARTISTS

Women are creative pioneers. Frida Kahlo was an artist with a distinctive style inspired by nature and traditional Mexican art. Kahlo only painted. . . didn't she?

Frida Kahlo

OH NO SHE DIDN'T!

Frida Kahlo is most famous for her colourful paintings, but she also created sculptures and wrote poetry. Through her vibrant art, she explored politics, culture, nature and identity.

Another creator of colourful compositions is Japanese artist Yayoi Kusama. Called the Princess of Polka Dots, she only uses polka dots in her artworks. . . doesn't she?

OH NO SHE DOESN'T!

Polka dots are definitely Kusama's speciality. For her, they symbolize infinity, Earth and memories of childhood.

When **Kusama** was a little girl, her mother had a polka-dotted kimono. But many other shapes, from square patchworks of colour to squiggly tendrils, fill Kusama's canvases, sculptures, films and performances.

Like Frida Kahlo, Kusama is herself a work of art. She often wears striking wigs, bold patterned clothing – and polka dots of course!

Yayoi Kusama

Chloe Wise

Chloe Wise is a Canadian artist who's famous for featuring food in her work. Wise's art explores consumerism, which is a strong desire to own possessions. In addition to food, she uses everyday objects and portraits of friends to explore this theme.

Did you know that Wise's rise to fame began with a bagel? She created realistic plastic sculptures of bread and made them look like designer bags. One of these was a bagel bag, which her friend, the actor Bobbi Menuez, wore to a fashion event. Everyone thought it was an exclusive designer bag – and wanted to have one. When people discovered it was actually a sculpture by Chloe Wise, the art world came calling!

Just in time for lunch!

25

WISE WORDSMITHS

Many classic books were written by women. For example, Jane Austen was a world-famous English novelist. She wrote light romances. . . didn't she?

OH NO SHE DIDN'T!

Novels like *Pride and Prejudice* include a love story or two, but Austen's books are actually clever critiques of society. Plots focus on female characters whose life choices were limited by the laws and expectations that society had for women at the time. Despite this, her heroines show intelligence and perseverance to earn their well-deserved happy endings.

Jane Austen

Many female authors wrote about social injustice.

Did you know that the English author **George Eliot** was a woman? Mary Ann Evans wrote under a man's name because in the mid-1800s women were usually expected to produce light-hearted stories. As George Eliot, she would be taken seriously, writing about topics that mattered to her.

George Eliot

By George, she can write!

The poet **Emily Dickinson** was born almost 200 years ago. Today she's seen as one of the most important American poets, but did you know that most of her poems were only discovered after she died? Her sister found them hidden in Dickinson's room and had them published.

Emily Dickinson

Beatrix Potter

I'm a bunny-fied star!

Some of the most beloved storybook characters were the work of women, such as Peter Rabbit, created by English writer **Beatrix Potter.**

Female authors have contributed so much to literature, but only adults are recognized for their writing. . . aren't they?

Did you know that Potter was also a naturalist? She loved the great outdoors and turned 4,000 acres of land into a national park!

OH NO THEY AREN'T!

Amanda Gorman

Amanda Gorman published her first book when she was seventeen! She's also the first National Youth Poet Laureate, a title granted to talented young poets in the United States. Gorman writes about equality and unity. She read her poem 'The Hill We Climb' at the inauguration of US President Biden.

DAZZLING DESIGNERS

Vera Wang is a Chinese-American fashion designer and business owner who has dressed politicians, film stars and athletes. Like many in her field she started her fashion company at an early age... didn't she?

OH NO SHE DIDN'T!

Vera Wang

Wang launched her clothing line in her forties, after several other careers. Wang had trained to be a figure skater since she was eight. When she didn't make it to the Olympic team, she left the sport to study art. After graduating, Wang worked as a fashion magazine editor and eventually became a designer for Ralph Lauren. She was inspired to launch her own designs when she got engaged. All of the wedding dresses seemed to be made for younger brides, so she created her own!

Wang has talked about her experience with ageism. She might have launched her fashion business later in life, but she doesn't let anything hold her back. Wang continues to grow and explore new interests, expanding her company into an empire that even includes desserts. For Vera Wang, success at any age is definitely sweet!

British Iraqi **Zaha Hadid** was a different type of designer. She was an architect, an award-winning designer of buildings. Often called the 'Queen of Curves', her designs are soaring masses of diagonal and curved shapes. They almost look alive – or like they're from outer space! The architecture company Hadid founded has designed almost 1,000 projects.

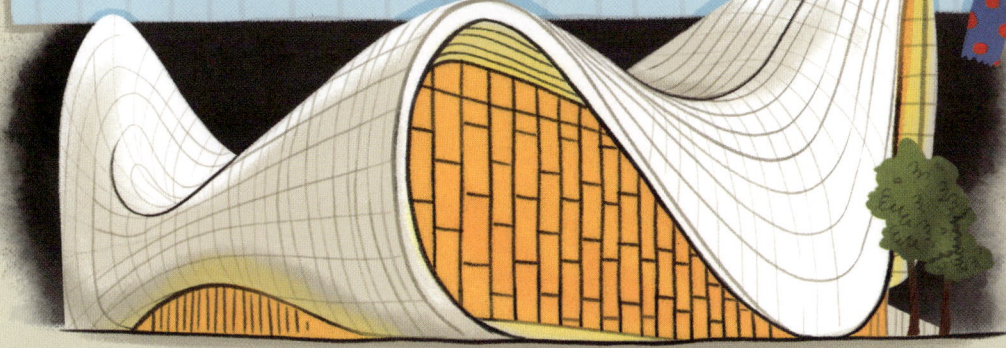

Hadid focused all her design talents on creating buildings. . . didn't she?

OH NO SHE DIDN'T!

Zaha Hadid

Hadid also designed furniture for her clients. And after she became a world-famous architect, she also designed several collections of shoes and bags! All of her work features the dramatic curves and unexpected shapes that characterize her architecture. Zaha Hadid was a true innovator!

MUSICAL MAESTROS

The world of classical music is full of contributions by women.

Florence Price was born in 1887, when much of the United States was racially segregated. Price faced discrimination both as an African American and as a woman. Nevertheless, she became a pianist, an organist, a teacher and a successful composer. She was the first African American woman to compose classical music played by a major orchestra.

After Price's death, she took her place among the classical greats. . . didn't she?

OH NO SHE DIDN'T!

Florence Price

Due to her race and gender, Price's music was largely unknown after her death, and was rarely played until recently.

Did you know that some of her compositions were almost lost? Fifty years after her death, dozens of Price's scores were found in an abandoned house.

Archivists at the University of Arkansas have preserved her works, allowing new generations to discover her music and write a history of classical music that includes women of colour.

Like Florence Price, **Nicola Benedetti** began studying music at an early age. Born in Scotland, Benedetti started playing violin when she was four years old. By eight, she was leading the National Children's Orchestra of Great Britain! Since then, Benedetti has won numerous awards, including a Grammy and two Classical BRIT Awards for Best Female Artist.

From violin strings to a string of awards...

Nicola Benedetti

Music hits the right keys to happiness!

In addition to being one of the most sought-after violinists, Benedetti has been recognized for her charitable work. The Benedetti Foundation aims to make music participation and appreciation available to all. To date they've reached thousands of people in more than 100 countries, through music lessons and live events.

Did you know that Nicola Benedetti is the first woman to lead the Edinburgh International Festival, a prestigious three-week arts festival in Scotland? She's not only a musical maestro, but an impressive orchestrator of events!

EDINBURGH INTERNATIONAL FESTIVAL

SUPERSTARS DAZZLING DIVAS

Beyoncé is one of the most successful entertainers ever. She was able to achieve success because she focused all of her energy on making music. . . didn't she?

OH NO SHE DIDN'T!

Beyoncé is so much more than a talented performer. She's a savvy businessperson who runs a number of companies, including a fashion label, several charities and her own music label.

Took me some time, but now I am strong.

Beyoncé is a self-made woman who's actively involved in all aspects of her career. Her global success has been won through hard work, dedication and a remarkable ability to set trends, instead of following them. There's good reason why people call her Queen Bey!

Beyoncé

Taylor Swift is another American superstar singer. She hired people to write most of her hit songs. . . didn't she?

OH NO SHE DIDN'T!

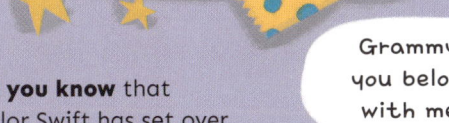
Taylor Swift

Taylor Swift has released her own versions of other people's songs, and she's co-written songs with other songwriters.

But the majority of her songs are ones that she wrote herself. In fact, Taylor Swift is considered to be one of the greatest songwriters of her generation. She's even written songs for other performers, including Miley Cyrus and Rihanna. Her concerts are so energetic that her 2023 show in Seattle shook the city with the force of a small earthquake!

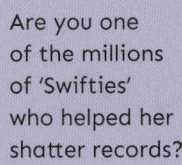

Did you know that Taylor Swift has set over fifty Guinness World Records? They're all for the incredible number of people who've bought, listened to, streamed, watched or downloaded her content.

Grammy, you belong with me!

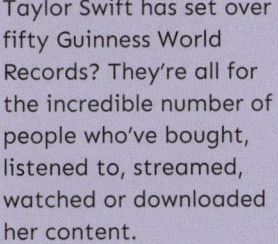

Are you one of the millions of 'Swifties' who helped her shatter records?

LEADING LADIES

Talented women have been at the centre of many blockbuster films, and the *Barbie* movie is one of the biggest. Australian actor Margot Robbie stars as the top-selling toy. She's so convincing as Barbie, it's no wonder the filmmakers always wanted her for the lead. . . didn't they?

GIRL POWER

OH NO THEY DIDN'T!

Margot Robbie

Greta Gerwig

As with many Hollywood films, several actors were considered before **Margot Robbie** was finally chosen. Once award-winning American director **Greta Gerwig** met her, it was clear Robbie was perfect for the part. The combination of Gerwig and Robbie, a stellar cast and a message of female empowerment tickled the world pink, making *Barbie* one of the highest-grossing films of all time!

Did you know that it is the first female-directed movie to make over £1 billion?

Michelle Yeoh is a superstar from Malaysia who's known as a martial arts expert. She studied martial arts from a young age. . . didn't she?

OH NO SHE DIDN'T!

Michelle Yeoh

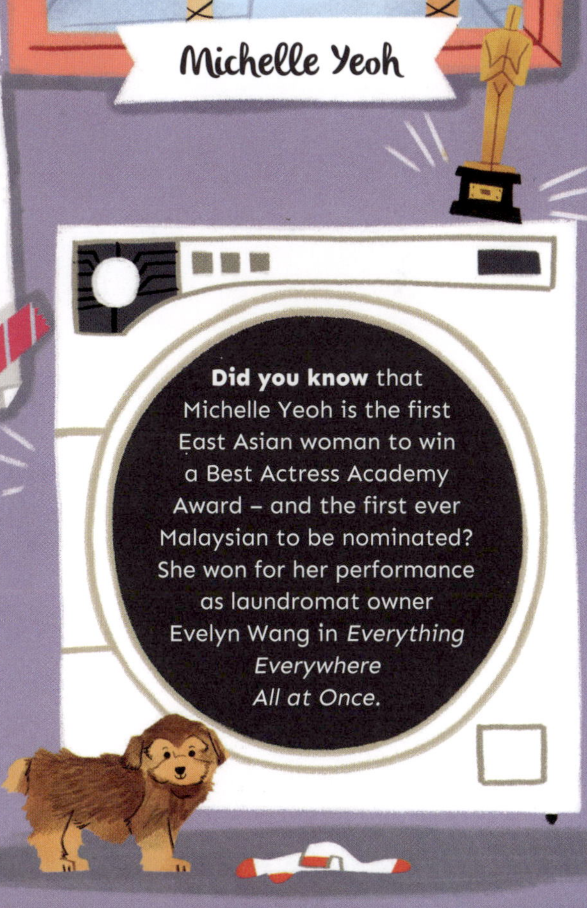

Despite performing her own stunts, **Yeoh** has never had formal martial arts training! She studied ballet at London's Royal Academy of Dance before becoming an actor. Yeoh learned her fierce moves while preparing for countless action-hero roles. She credits dance training for the flexibility and agility needed to quickly pick up fighting techniques. She must have a black belt in ballet!

Did you know that Michelle Yeoh is the first East Asian woman to win a Best Actress Academy Award – and the first ever Malaysian to be nominated? She won for her performance as laundromat owner Evelyn Wang in *Everything Everywhere All at Once*.

SCREEN SENSATIONS

Jenna Ortega is an American actor who has graced movie screens, TV screens – and touch screens, too. As a successful performer, Ortega is an extrovert. . . isn't she?

> Wednesday, evermore!

Jenna Ortega

OH NO SHE ISN'T!

Ortega calls herself a 'massive introvert', a trait she shares with Wednesday Addams, the gothy misfit with dazzling dance moves she plays on the show *Wednesday*. She uses her fame to support diversity, equal rights and organisations that encourage young people to become change makers.

MILLIE BOBBY BROWN

British actor Millie Bobby Brown, on the other hand, is an extrovert. She has a lot in common with Eleven, the mysterious character with superhuman powers she plays on *Stranger Things*. . . doesn't she?

OH NO SHE DOESN'T!

Brown admits she finds the slightly scary Eleven very intense. She has much more in common with Enola Holmes, the playful, down-to-earth teenager she plays in the *Enola Holmes* films, who is the younger sister of detective Sherlock Holmes.

Did you know that Brown is partially deaf? The disability can make her job as an actor difficult. She teamed up with colleagues to give her visual cues on set so she could focus on delivering award-winning performances.

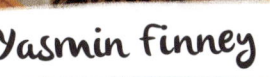
Yasmin Finney

Yasmin Finney is one of the breakout stars of the hit series *Heartstopper*, wowing fans and critics alike for her portrayal of Elle. Like Elle, Finney is a transgender woman.

She first became known for her honest social media posts about life as a young, Black, British trans woman.

Did you know that Finney was unhoused for a period when she was very young? Despite living in poverty and facing discrimination, Finney's determination has seen her rise up as a timeless star. . . literally! In 2023, she played the first trans character in the time-travelling TV series *Doctor Who!*

MEDIA MOGULS

Oprah Winfrey is an African American superstar who is also a media mogul: the founder and owner of a media empire that spans books, film, TV, podcasts and more. She's one of the first Black female billionaires and uses her fortune to promote female empowerment, education and equality. Oprah Winfrey credits her grandmother, Hattie Mae Lee, for raising her to be confident. Winfrey has approached every aspect of her life with confidence. . . hasn't she?

OH NO SHE HASN'T!

Oprah Winfrey

Oprah Winfrey, the Queen of Media!

Oprah Winfrey is open about her struggles with weight and its impact on her self-esteem. People treat her differently when she's heavier. Winfrey is one of many women who promote body positivity, appreciating all body types rather than accepting one standard of beauty and health.

Another American media mogul is the Queen of Country, **Dolly Parton.** Parton is one of the best-selling music artists of all time and a super-successful actor, songwriter and executive. Parton owns a music publishing company, a production company, a theme park and a literacy foundation that's given away more than 200 million books to children around the world!

Like Oprah Winfrey, Dolly Parton grew up in poverty. She studied music and songwriting. . . didn't she?

Dolly Parton

OH NO SHE DIDN'T!

DOLLY PARTON

I WILL AWAYS LOVE YOU

Over 20 million copies sold!

Parton came from a musical family. She never had formal musical training, though, and discovered her talents while singing in church. When she was seven, Parton taught herself how to play guitar from an instrument made from broken parts! From these modest beginnings rose a legend.

Did you know that Parton wrote one of the top-selling songs ever? It's called 'I Will Always Love You'. We will always love Dolly Parton!

LEADERS
LEADING LIGHTS

Women have served as elected leaders of many nations. Iceland is home to the first democratically elected female president ever, Vigdís Finnbogadóttir. Decades later, Jóhanna Sigurðardóttir became the first female prime minister in Iceland, as well as the first openly queer person elected as head of government anywhere in the world!

Vigdís
Finnbogadóttir

During her time as prime minister Sigurðardóttir focused on gender equality, passing laws to protect the rights of women and reducing the gender pay gap. Sigurðardóttir always wanted a career in politics. . . didn't she?

Jóhanna
Sigurðardóttir

OH NO SHE DIDN'T!

Sigurðardóttir's first job after graduating from university was as a flight attendant. She was very active in the labor unions that represented cabin crew and found herself drawn to politics as a result, flying to heights she never dreamt of before.

Indira Gandhi was the first female prime minister of India. Her father, Jawaharlal Nehru, became India's first prime minister when the nation won its independence from the British Empire. Gandhi followed her father into politics and was elected president of their political party. In 1966, Gandhi was elected prime minister. During eleven years in office, Gandhi proved herself to be a strong leader. Her policies were frequently controversial but she is often credited with modernizing India.

Indira Gandhi came from a family of politicians who fought for India's independence. They counted the activist and lawyer known as Mahatma Gandhi as a relative. . . didn't they?

OH NO THEY DIDN'T!

Indira Gandhi

Mahatma Gandhi knew Indira Gandhi's father and her husband Feroze Ghandy, but they were not related. Ghandhy changed the spelling of his surname to Gandhi to honour the famed peace activist.

FORMIDABLE FIRST LADIES

Women have had considerable influence in government – not just as prime minister or president, but while serving their country as first ladies. Eva Perón, known affectionately as Evita, was the wife of Argentinian president Juan Perón. Her father was a wealthy rancher, and her family grew up in comfort. . . didn't they?

Eva Perón

OH NO THEY DIDN'T!

Perón's father left her family when she was only a year old. Her rise from a life of poverty through talent and determination has inspired millions! As first lady, Perón created a charity to help the poor, and she supported women's right to vote. Perón's life as a magnetic first lady who captured the hearts of the world has been celebrated in biographies, films and a popular stage musical.

Michelle Obama

Michelle Obama is the first African American first lady of the United States. Like Perón, she was a strong presence during her husband's presidency. She advocated for a wide range of causes from LGBTQ+ rights to nutrition and health, and supporting military families.

Michelle Obama has a law degree. Most first ladies of the United States earned post-graduate degrees. . . didn't they?

OH NO THEY DIDN'T!

While many American first ladies had a college education, Obama is one of five to have a master's degree. Laura Bush, Jill Biden, and Hillary Clinton are others.

Did you know that Michelle Obama is a best-selling author? Her autobiography *Becoming* has sold almost 20 million copies around the world! And she's become a media mogul alongside her husband, with a production company that produces podcasts and films programmes to 'entertain, inform and inspire – while elevating new and diverse voices'.

REGAL ROYALTY

Queen Elizabeth I is one of history's most memorable monarchs. During her forty-five-year reign, England became a superpower. She achieved this despite facing discrimination. Many people at the time thought a woman couldn't be a capable ruler.

Elizabeth I was a supporter of the arts. She and the famous playwright William Shakespeare were good friends and often attended performances of his plays together. . . didn't they?

OH NO THEY DIDN'T!

With skull in hand, art thou a writer or a gravedigger?

A writer – a dead good one!

Queen Elizabeth 1

It's true that **Queen Elizabeth** loved theatre, and Shakespeare's company performed at court, so it's likely they were introduced. But Queen Elizabeth and Shakespeare weren't BFFs. They weren't even pen pals.

Cleopatra, the last pharaoh of Ancient Egypt, is another queen who supported the arts. She promoted Egyptian culture through her patronage of artists and building projects. Her reign covered a perilous period when her kingdom was taken over by the Roman Empire. She aimed to protect her kingdom by using her main asset, her beauty. . . didn't she?

I'll take brains over beauty.

OH NO SHE DIDN'T!

Cleopatra

No one knows what **Cleopatra** looked like. She might have been beautiful, but her allure came from within. Ancient writers praised her charm and wit. She spoke many languages and was an expert politician. Whatever Cleopatra's appearance, intelligence was the asset that made her a formidable ruler.

A wit quicker than any snake!

The last queen of France was Marie Antoinette, who was executed in 1793. When confronted about the extreme poverty in her kingdom, being told that they had no bread to eat, she replied, 'Let them eat cake!'. . . didn't she?

I prefer a cup of hot chocolate.

OH NO SHE DIDN'T!

The quote comes from a book by the philosopher Jean-Jacques Rousseau, written five years before **Marie Antoinette** was queen! It was many years later that the quote was linked to the queen.

POLITICAL POWERHOUSES

Constance Markievicz was the first woman elected to Parliament in the UK. She was passionate about women's suffrage and independence for Ireland, and she used her position in government to advocate for these issues. . . didn't she?

OH NO SHE DIDN'T!

CONSTANCE MARKIEVICZ

While Markievicz's election in 1918 was a first for a woman, she didn't take her seat. Many elected officials in Ireland did the same, as an act of protest against the UK government. When Ireland became independent in 1921, **Markievicz** served as Minister of Labour for the new country, making her one of the first ever female government ministers in the world!

I'm standing up for our rights!

Suffrage is a family affair!

EMMELINE PANKHURST

Women in the UK were granted the right to vote in 1918. The suffragette **Emmeline Pankhurst** was a key figure in the fight for equality at the polls.
Did you know that Pankhurst joined the suffragist cause at the age of just fourteen, when her mother took her to her first meeting?

JEANNETTE RANKIN

Like Constance Markiewicz, the first woman to serve in the United States Congress was a vocal advocate for woman's rights. **Jeannette Rankin** from Montana was elected to the House of Representatives in 1916.

Did you know that when Rankin was elected, many women in the United States couldn't vote? Four years later, in 1920, the 19th Amendment to the US Constitution granted most female citizens the right to vote, although many women were still prevented from doing so by local laws, especially women of colour.

Women should be able to vote.

Jacinda Ardern

Jacinda Ardern, one of the youngest ever prime ministers, entered politics while she was still in school. Ardern was pregnant with her daughter while serving as prime minister of New Zealand. She had to quit her job to focus on being a mother. . . didn't she?

OH NO SHE DIDN'T!

After leaving the government in the care of a deputy during her six-week maternity leave, **Ardern** skillfully juggled motherhood and her career. She was an inspiration to working mothers and is remembered for championing equality and diversity.

TRAILBLAZERS FEARLESS FIRSTS

The world famous American pilot Amelia Earhart was the first woman to pilot a plane solo across the Atlantic. In 1937 Earhart attempted to fly around the world with her navigator Fred Noonan, but their aircraft disappeared over the Pacific Ocean. They didn't really disappear, though. Earhart and Noonan were spies. They went into hiding. . . didn't they?

OH NO THEY DIDN'T!

There's no evidence Earhart and Noonan were spies. The theory came about because their plane vanished near Japanese-controlled territory. Relations between the United States and Japan were very strained in the years leading up to World War II.

Because Earhart was a friend of President Franklin Roosevelt and his wife, Eleanor Roosevelt, some people wondered if the President hired his pilot friend to spy on the Japanese. What really happened to Earhart and Noonan remains a mystery!

Amelia Earhart

Junko Tabei was the first woman to climb Earth's highest mountain, Mount Everest – and the first woman to complete the Seven Summits challenge by climbing the highest peak on all seven continents. Born in Japan, Tabei was an energetic child who effortlessly took to climbing. . . didn't she?

OH NO SHE DIDN'T!

Tabei wasn't an athletic child. She never thought about climbing until a school trip to Mount Nasu made her appreciate the beauty of the mountains. It wasn't easy to pursue her hobby, though. Tabei's parents didn't have money to pay for the expensive sport, and climbing clubs were for men.

Junko Tabei

Despite discrimination and the high cost of climbing, Tabei broke records while advocating for the preservation of mountaintop habitats and writing seven books about her love of the world's highest places.

WILDERNESS WARRIORS

British zoologist Jane Goodall is a pioneer in primate research and habitat conservation. She spent sixty years observing chimpanzees in the wild and concluded that they had very little in common with humans. . . didn't she?

OH NO SHE DIDN'T!

We're all bananas for Jane Goodall!

Jane Goodall

Goodall discovered that humans aren't the only animals who make and use tools. She also revealed that chimps are individuals with unique personalities – just like us!

Many male researchers dismissed Goodall's work, believing female scientists too emotional to make logical conclusions. Jane Goodall proved them wrong! Her discoveries changed the way we look at the natural world – and ourselves.

Another eco-warrior who researched primates was American Dian Fossey. Fossey's ground-breaking work in Rwanda proved that gorillas are complex, social animals – not the monsters books and films portray them to be. Fossey was devoted to protecting her beloved gorillas' habitat. She developed a love for animals early in life because she had a lot of pets. . . didn't she?

Dian Fossey

OH NO SHE DIDN'T!

The only pet Fossey's parents permitted was a goldfish! It was through horseback riding that she developed a bond with animals.

Did you know that Fossey won a number of awards as a young rider?

Healing the Earth one tree at a time.

Wangari Maathai

Many women have led movements to protect the planet. **Wangari Maathai** founded the Green Belt Movement in Kenya. This organization fights deforestation by planting trees while training women to lead sustainability programmes.

Did you know that Maathai was the first African woman to win the Nobel Peace Prize? She was also the author of many books about Africa and the Earth. Maathai did much more than just plant trees. She sowed the seeds of conservation and equality.

DARING DEFENDERS

Not all trailblazers are adults. Pakistan-born Malala Yousafzai is the youngest person to receive a Nobel Peace Prize. She was just seventeen when she accepted the prize in recognition of her courageous advocacy for girls' education. Two years earlier, Yousafzai had survived an assassination attempt by the Taliban, which disagreed with her views. After the attack, Yousafzai moved to the UK to live a quiet life. . . didn't she?

Malala Yousafzai

OH NO SHE DIDN'T!

Yousafzai is still a daring defender of freedom and equality today. The organisation Malala Fund, which she co-founded, raises money and awareness to help every girl receive an education.

Greta Thunberg has been an environmental activist since she was fifteen! Born in Sweden, she inspired students around the world to stage protests calling for action on climate change. Since then, Thunberg has addressed the United Nations Climate Change Conference and numerous governments. She's written books and continues to fight for legislation to protect our planet.

Did you know that Greta Thunberg has autism? It's a condition that can make it difficult to interact with others. Thunberg has said that she's sometimes a bit different from other people, but that 'being different is a superpower'. That makes Thunberg a superhero!

Greta Thunberg

Jazz Jennings

Jazz Jennings is another young defender. At the age of thirteen, she founded the company Purple Rainbow Tails that made dress-up mermaid tails to raise money for transgender children. Jennings has won many awards for her work as an activist defending the rights of transgender youth.

Did you know Jennings is also a TV star? She was the voice for an animated transgender singer and also a magical fairy!

SPORT STARS

American tennis stars Venus and Serena Williams are trailblazing players. They have numerous Olympic medals and Gram Slam tennis titles, both as individual players and as doubles teammates.

The sisters' record-breaking careers challenged stereotypes in a sport that wasn't particularly diverse at the time. Their awesome skill drew people of colour to the court, inspiring young athletes from different backgrounds to become professional players.

Venus and Serena Williams

The Williams sisters were both ranked number 1 at different times and played against each other thirty-one times! They became fierce rivals both on and off the court. . . didn't they?

OH NO THEY DIDN'T!

Despite their on-court rivalry, the Williams sisters have always been close.

Together they contributed to a film about their father (who was their coach) and their early days playing tennis as kids. And they both use their celebrity to fight discrimination and the gender pay gap in sport.

Leah Williamson is a professional footballer who is captain of the Lionesses, the national women's team for England. She led the team to stardom and their first ever UEFA European Championship victory in 2022.

Like the Williams sisters, Williamson is a role model for young athletes. She was the first England women's footballer to address the United Nations and has been a vocal supporter of LGBTQ+ rights.

Kicking goals for equality!

Did you know that Williamson almost dropped out of football once? After seeing Greg Rutherford win a gold medal for the long jump at the 2012 Summer Olympics in London, she considered switching to track and field. It's no wonder Leah Williamson has been able to jump so many hurdles to become one of football's brightest stars!

TIMELINE

Remarkable women have been a part of human history since the beginning, from timeless legendary figures to modern-day role models and superstars. Travel through time with them!

Isis

Oshun

1596
Pocahontas

1533
Elizabeth I

1412
Joan of Arc

1755
Marie Antoinette

1775
Jane Austen

1815
Ada Lovelace

1918
Katherine Johnson

1917
Indira Gandhi

1914
Hedy Lamarr

1910
Dorothy Vaughan

1907
Frida Kahlo

1919
Eva Perón

1921
Mary Jackson

1929
Yayoi Kusama

1930
Vigdís Finnbogadóttir

1932
Dian Fossey

1980
Jacinda Ardern

1977
Samantha Cristoforetti

1964
Michelle Obama

1964
Jennifer Doudna

1962
Michelle Yeoh

1980
Venus Williams

1981
Serena Williams

1981
Beyoncé

1983
Greta Gerwig

1987
Nicola Benedetti

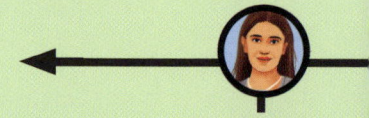

2004
Millie Bobby Brown

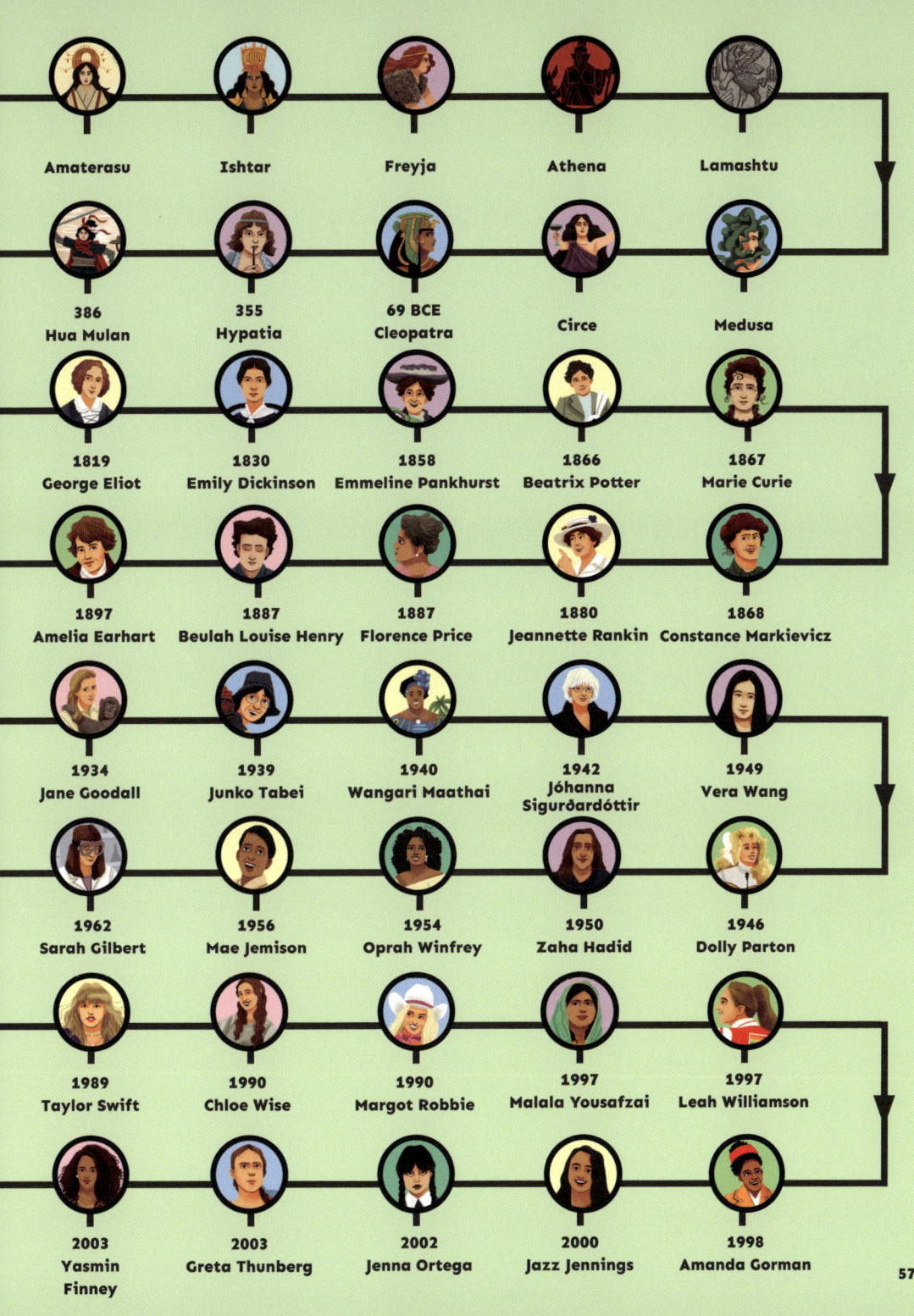

Amaterasu

Ishtar

Freyja

Athena

Lamashtu

386
Hua Mulan

355
Hypatia

69 BCE
Cleopatra

Circe

Medusa

1819
George Eliot

1830
Emily Dickinson

1858
Emmeline Pankhurst

1866
Beatrix Potter

1867
Marie Curie

1897
Amelia Earhart

1887
Beulah Louise Henry

1887
Florence Price

1880
Jeannette Rankin

1868
Constance Markievicz

1934
Jane Goodall

1939
Junko Tabei

1940
Wangari Maathai

1942
Jóhanna
Sigurðardóttir

1949
Vera Wang

1962
Sarah Gilbert

1956
Mae Jemison

1954
Oprah Winfrey

1950
Zaha Hadid

1946
Dolly Parton

1989
Taylor Swift

1990
Chloe Wise

1990
Margot Robbie

1997
Malala Yousafzai

1997
Leah Williamson

2003
Yasmin
Finney

2003
Greta Thunberg

2002
Jenna Ortega

2000
Jazz Jennings

1998
Amanda Gorman

MAP

Have a look at where in the world each of these remarkable women were born. No matter where they're from, they've all made a global impact.

WEST COAST USA

Dian Fossey
San Francsico, CA

Greta Gerwig
Sacramento, CA

Amanda Gorman
Los Angeles, CA

Venus Williams
Lynwood, CA

Jenna Ortega
Palm Desert, CA

**Vigdís Finnbogadóttir,
Jóhanna Sigurðardóttir**
Reykjavik, Iceland

Freyja
Scandinavia

**Samantha
Cristoforett**
Milan, Italy

Jennifer Doudna
Washington, D.C.

Serena Williams
Saginaw, MI

**Emily
Dickinson**
Amherst, MA

Pocahontas
Werowocomoco,
VA

Joan of Arc
Domrémy-la-Pucelle,
France

Jeannette Rankin
Missoula, MT

**Millie Bobby
Brown**
Marbella,
Spain

Michelle Obama
Chicago, IL

Vera Wang
NYC

Amelia Earhart
Atchison, KS

Taylor Swift
West Reading, PA

Isis
Egypt

Dorothy Vaughan
Kansas City, MO

Beyoncé
Houston, TX

Chloe Wise
Montreal, Canada

Mary Jackson
Hampton, VA

Marie Antoinette
Vienna, Austria

Oshun
SW Nigeria

SOUTHERN USA

Katherine Johnson
White Sulphur Springs, WV

Oprah Winfrey
Kosciusko, MS

Eva Péron
Los Toldos,
Argentina

**Cleopatra,
Hypatia**
Alexandria, Egypt

Florence Price
Little Rock, AR

Jazz Jennings
South Florida

Beulah Louise Henry
Raleigh, NC

Dolly Parton
Pittman Center, TN

Mae Jemison
Decatur, AL

Frida Kahlo
Mexico City,
Mexico

UK

Yasmin Finney
Manchester

Jane Goodall
Hampstead, London

Jane Austen
Steventon

Leah Williamson
Milton Keynes

**Constance
Markievicz**
Buckingham Gate

Elizabeth I
Greenwich, London

Sarah Gilbert
Kettering

George Eliot
Warwickshire

Beatrix Potter
London

Nicola Benedetti
Scotland

Ada Lovelace
London

Emmeline Pankhurst
Manchester

Greta Thunberg
Stockholm, Sweden

Hedy Lamarr
Vienna, Austria

Marie Curie
Warsaw, Poland

Zaha Hadid
Baghdad, Iraq

**Ishtar,
Lamashtu**
Mesopotamia

Amaterasu
Japan

Hua Mulan
China

Junko Tabei
Miharu, Japan

Yayoi Kusama
Matsumoto, Japan

**Malala
Yousafzai**
Mingora,
Pakistan

**Indira
Gandhi**
Prayagraj,
India

Wangari Maathai
Ihithe, Kenya

Jacinda Ardern
Hamilton, NZ

Michelle Yeoh
Ipoh, Malaysia

Athena
Greece

Medusa
Greece

Circe
Greece

Margot Robbie
Dalby, Australia

GLOSSARY

Academy Award (also called an **Oscar**) an award given out annually by the Academy of Motion Picture Arts and Sciences to honour excellence in the film industry.

ageism discrimination or prejudice against people based on their age.

Ancient Egypt an ancient civilization in northern Africa known for advancements in mathematics, science, art and architecture – in particular the huge pyramids they built.

autism a condition that affects the way someone sees and understands the world, sometimes making it difficult to relate to other people.

biochemistry the study of chemical reactions in living things.

body positivity the acceptance of your own body and the bodies of others in all shapes and sizes.

deforestation the process of clearing trees for building, farming or other human needs.

diversity differences between people and cultures, and the celebration of these differences.

divinity a god or goddess.

DNA the chemical molecule that contains all the genetic information about a living organism.

empowerment encouraging and supporting people to believe in themselves and pursue their dreams.

first lady the wife of a president or ruler of a nation.

folk hero a person, either historic or legendary, whose life story is embraced and beloved by a culture or group.

foundation a charitable organization set up to help people or causes.

gender pay gap the difference in money paid to men and women who do the same job.

gene editing a scientific procedure for changing the DNA of a living organism.

glass ceiling a concept that describes an invisible limit set by prejudice, which prevents women or minority groups from reaching past a certain level in their career.

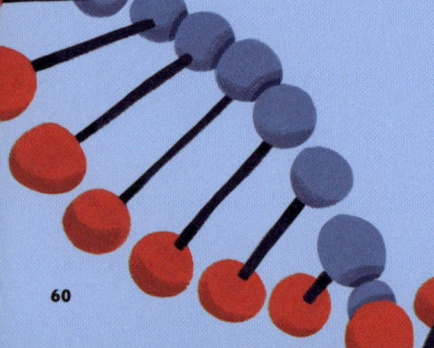

Guinness World Record a global achievement that makes up part of a list published annually in a book of the same name.

International Space Station (ISS) a spacecraft orbiting Earth, where astronauts from around the world work and live.

introvert someone who enjoys spending time alone in a quiet, peaceful place.

legend a mythical person or a historic figure whose life is a larger-than-life mix of fact and fiction.

media mogul a person who runs a large entertainment company or a group of companies that focus on media.

Mesopotamia an area in West Asia, centred in modern-day Iraq, where some of the world's first civilizations began.

monarch the hereditary ruler of a country or empire.

music publishing the business of selling printed or recorded music and distributing the money earned from it.

Nobel Peace Prize a prestigious award presented annually to people around the world who have worked to promote peace and justice.

pacifist someone who doesn't believe in violence or war.

parliament a name for an elected law-making organization in many countries around the world.

pathogen an organism that causes disease; pathogens are often called germs.

primate a member of the group of mammals that includes monkeys, apes and humans.

prime minister the head of government in countries with a parliamentary system, such as the UK or Japan.

Roman Empire an ancient civilization centred around the Mediterranean Sea known for its advancements in sciences, philosophy and art.

segregate to keep different people apart, such as people of different races, for reasons of discrimination.

Seven Summits a mountaineering achievement consisting of climbing the highest mountain on each continent.

Slavic referring to the culture and language of certain Eastern and Central European people.

social justice the concept that everyone should have the same rights and access to opportunities and success.

suffragette a woman who fought for the right to vote.

sustainability the idea of living in harmony with the planet, using resources responsibly to protect the world for future generations.

UEFA (short for **Union of European Football Associations**) the official organization that governs football in Europe.

vaccinology the study of creating vaccines that provide protection from diseases.

Walk of Fame a famous section of a street in Hollywood, California, with stars on the sidewalk dedicated to notable people in entertainment.

x-ray a technique that uses energy in the form of radiation that allows doctors to take photos of bones and organs inside the body.

Women really are remarkable, aren't they?

ABOUT THE AUTHOR

Eric Huang was born in New Jersey and grew up in California. He loved mythology, nature, comic books and more than anything else. . . dinosaurs. When Eric went to college he studied paleontology, hoping to find fossils. But life took him all the way to Australia, where he found kangaroos and koalas instead. Since then, Eric has worked with Disney, Penguin Books and LEGO – and found a few fossils along the way. He now teaches at City, University of London, writes books and makes podcasts.

Acknowlededgments

Thank you to Holly, Alice, and Nancy for all of your invaluable feedback. Thank you Shannon for signing up this series. And thanks to Angela, Brian, Elias, Emma, Lynsey, Nic, and my mom for pushing me to write!

Eric Huang

ABOUT THE ILLUSTRATOR

Sam Caldwell is an illustrator based in Glasgow where he lives with his wife and two cats: Tonks and Luna. Sam loves inventing characters and creating images packed full of detail, texture and coluor. He is passionate about animals and nature, and when he's not drawing, Sam can often be found exploring the Scottish Highlands. He has illustrated many books for children, including the award-winning *Do Bears Poop in the Woods*?

Acknowlededgments

A big thanks to Kat and Susi for all of the fantastic design work and steering of the ship on this series. Thank you also Doreen, Kate and Tom for the opportunity and continued support.

Sam Caldwell